108 Drops of Mindful Quotes from Social Media

For the Therapist, Client and Anyone Looking for Calm

By Omileye E Achikeobi – Lewis

A Naked Truth Book

UK, United States

A Naked Truth Book

P. O. Box 461

South Carolina, SC 29720

www.yeyeosun.com

Copyright © 2014 Omileye Achikeobi-Lewis

Design by: Omileye Achikeobi-Lewis & L. Derrick Lewis

All rights reserved. This book or parts thereof, may Not be reproduced in any form without permission

This book is printed in the United States of America

May 2014 Copyright © 2014 Omileye Achikeobi-Lewis

All rights reserved.

9780954206680

Library of Congress Number: 2014909713

I would like to dedicate this book to all who are looking for peace.

When people have peace in themselves, then there can be peace in the world.

-Thich Nhat Hahn

CONTENTS

Introduction   10
Omileye Achikeobi-Lewis

Mindful Quotes   12-119

Mindful Reference Table   120-121

My Mindful Quotes   122-141

Acknowledgements

I would like to thank all who have supported me along this journey, and all who posted so many wonderful inspirational mindful quotes on Facebook and Social Media to uplift the world.

Introduction

The intention of this mindfulness quotes book is to help the counseling therapist and their client have mindful quotes to hand which can help facilitate a therapeutic journey towards wholeness. Any individual looking for a way to live more mindfully will also find this book useful.

Why this book?

I did not plan to write this book, but it seems as though it sprung from the depths of Wise Mind's illuminations. One day, bored and down about life I sat browsing my Facebook. As I did so I noticed my mood began to slowly change for the better. I wondered why? Then it suddenly hit me, I had spent most of my time looking at the many positive quotes posted by friend and family on my Facebook. It was then that I realized that Facebook and social media played an important role in inspiring millions on a daily basis.

A few days after this experience I had a deep urge to collect and publish as many Facebook and social media quotes as possible that inspired mindful living. Eventually I took the idea seriously when one day, for my internship at the Catawba Community Mental Health Center, I began to help lead the mindfulness segment of their DBT (Dialectical Behavior Therapy) group. On the first day of group Summer Smith, the facilitator, asked each person to bring quotes from their Facebook and social media along to each group session as part of a mindfulness activity. Since I had already thought about collecting and documenting, in book form, positive mindful quotes from Facebook and social, Smith's request felt like a sign that I should go ahead and follow my heart. I felt further spurred on when I saw the powerful transformative effective the mindful positive quotes collected from Facebook and Social media had on the DBT group.

What is Mindfulness?

In his book *Mindfulness for Beginners* Jon Kabat-Zinn (2003), states mindfulness is, "the awareness that emerges through paying attention on purpose, in the present moment non-judgmentally to the unfolding of experience moment by moment" (p. 145). Mindfulness helps us act from the calm waters of Wise Mind, as opposed to the bi waves of Emotional Mind. We can act from Wise Mind by learning how to stop, breathe, observe, and bring ourselves into the present moment. As we do so we can observe our thoughts and feelings in a non-judgmental manner. Thoughts that do not serve us in a positive way can be replaced by ones that do. The quotes in this book help us to do so.

How to Use the Book?

The 108 mindful quotes in this book equals the number of beads in a meditation prayer rosary. The quotes help us to mindfully focus on positive thoughts that help equip us with positive coping skills and life results. The book can be used individually or in a group setting. You can locate quotes relevant to a situation by going to the Quotes Reference Table, and you can have fun adding your own mindful quotes in the My Mindful Quotes section. It is my deepest wish that we all live rich, mindful and whole lives.

SINCE EVERYTHING IS A REFLECTIONOF OUR MIND

Then everything can be changed by the mind.

-Buddha

EMPTY your mind, be formless, shapeless, like water. If you put water into a cup, it becomes the cup. You put water into a bottle and it becomes the bottle. You put it in a teapot, it becomes the teapot. Now, water can flow or it can crash. Be water, my friend.

-Bruce Lee

DISCOVERY COMES
NOT IN SEEKING <u>NEW LAND</u>
BUT WITH SEEING
WITH <u>NEW EYES.</u>

-Marcel Proust

"If you are searching for that person that will change your life, take a look in the mirror"

Author Unknown

Life begins
AT THE END OF YOUR
COMFORT ZONE.

-Neale Donald Walsh

Purpose is the reason you journey. Passion is the fire that lights your WAY.

-Author unknown

Better than a thousand hollow words is ONE WORD that brings peace.

-Buddha

SOMETIMES GOD SENDS
MIRACLES THAT SEEM SO SMALL
THAT YOU MAY NOT NOTICE THEM
STRAIGHT AWAY.
BUT THEY WILL ADD UP
TO MAKING
BIG POSITIVE CHANGES FOR YOU.

-Doreen Virtue

She liked planting seeds
and said,
"Another NEW DAY to begin again.
LET YOUR soul sit
in the driver's seat
and
give you a ride of a life time,
for a lifetime."

-Miranda Rhondeau

Every moment of our existence holds an infinite number of possibilities.

-Wayne Dyer

The best things in life are free. That is just about the oldest, most trite, most hackneyed "saying"
You could come across today. But it is so, so true.
And it is important never to lose sight of that. So look around you. Wherever you see friendship, loyalty, laughter, love...there is your treasure.

-     -Neale Walsh, Conversations with God

Spend your time with people
who want only the very best for you,
and be someone who wants only the
very best for others too.

-Cheryl Richardson

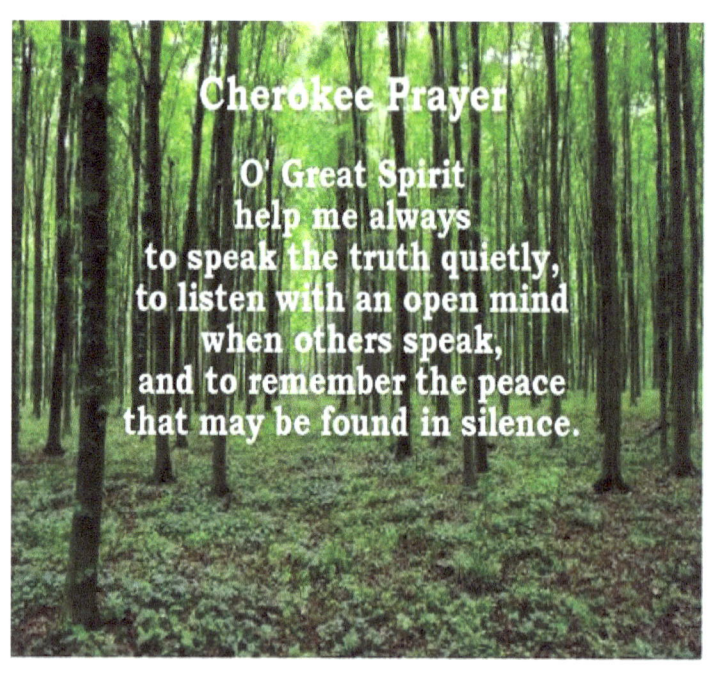

If you
cannot
be positive,
then at least
be quiet.

-Joel Osteen

*I am realistic,
I EXPECT miracles.*

-Wayne Dyer

> WE ARE FASCINATED
> BY THE WORDS
> BUT WHERE WE MEET
> IS IN THE SILENCE
> BETWEEN THEM
>
> — RAM DASS

You will never change your life until you change something you do daily. The secret of your success is found in your daily routine.

-John C. Maxwell

Open hearts. See
    LOVE everywhere…..

    -Author Unknown

Empty space
Is where the chi is.

-Lee Holden

If I waited for perfection
I would <u>never</u> write a word.

-Margaret Atwood

YOU CANNOT BE lonely if
YOU LIKE THE PERSON you're
alone with.

-Wayne Dyer

Listen and Silence are
Spelt with the
same letters…think about it. :)

-Unknown

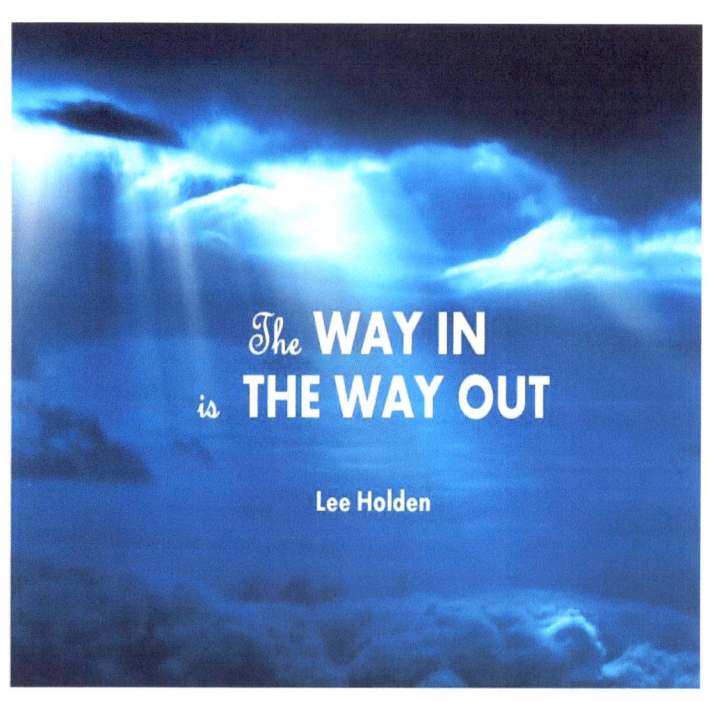

THE GREATEST MINDFULNESS IS IN THE HEART.

-Derrick Lewis

Just when the caterpillar
Thought that life
was over
It became a
Butterfly.

-Author unknown

TRUST IN YOUR
OWN MAGNIFICENCE.

-Wayne Dyer

You can't stop the waves
but you can learn to surf.

-John Kabat Zinn

While one may encounter many defeats, one must not be defeated.

-Maya Angelou

People say nothing is impossible, but I do nothing every day.

-Winnie the Pooh

THE COMFORT ZONE IS A BEAUTIFUL PLACE BUT NOTHING GOOD LIVES THERE.

-Author unknown

It is always our own self we find
at the end of the journey.

The sooner we face that self, the
better.

-Ella Maillart

Peace.
It does not mean to be in a place where there is no noise, trouble or hard work. It means to be in the midst of those things and *still be calm in your heart.*

-Author unknown

SOMETIMES SURRENDER MEANS GIVING UP TRYING TO *understand* and being comfortable with not knowing.

-Eckhart Tolle

No one can steal your peace without your permission.

-Cheryl Richardson

The only limits you have
are the limits
you *believe.*

-Wayne Dyer

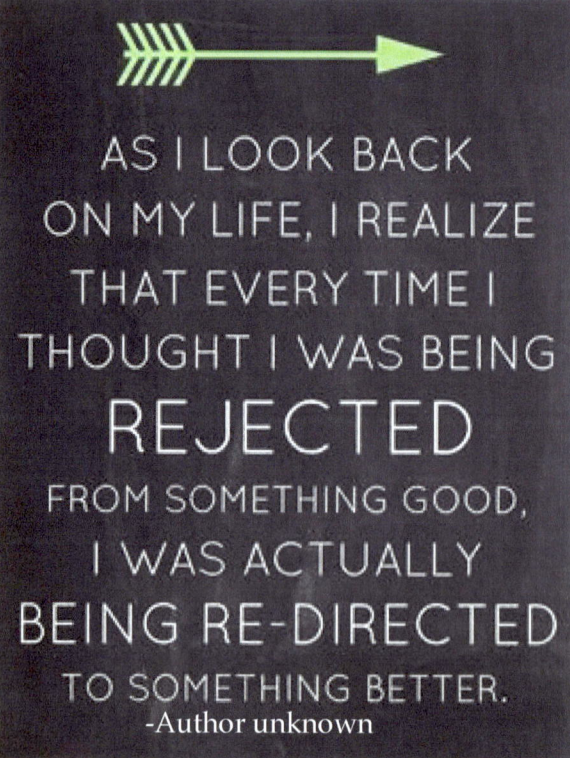

I have a past
    but I don't
live there anymore.

-Author unknown

Sometimes the wrong train can take us to the right place.

-Paulo Coelho

The present moment is the only moment available to us, and it is the doorway to all moments.

-Thich Nhat Hahn

IF YOU ARE ALIVE there is a purpose FOR YOUR LIFE.

-Rick Warren

God is the friend of silence.

-Mother Teresa

Every breath we take, every step we make, can be filled with peace, joy and serenity.

-Thich Nhat Hanh

When we are no longer able to change a situation, we are challenged to change ourselves.

-Viktor Frankl

He who has a why to live for can bear almost any how.

-Friedrich Nietzsche

The last of the human freedoms is the ability to choose one's attitude in any given set of circumstances.

-Viktor Frankl

Sleep is the best meditation.

-Dalai Lama

But there was no need to be ashamed of tears, for tears bore witness that a man had the greatest of courage, the courage to suffer.

-Viktor Frankl

In some ways suffering ceases to be suffering at the moment it finds a meaning.

-Viktor Frankl

We must be conscious of EACH BREATH, each movement, every thought and feeling, everything that has a relation to ourselves.

-Thich Nhat Hahn

Tread softly,
Breathe Deeply,
Laugh Hysterically.

-Nelson Mandela

I can be **changed** *by what happens to me. I refuse to be* **reduced** *by it.*

-Maya Angelou

LAUGH AS LONG AS YOU BREATHE,
and love as long as you live.

-Johnny Depp

Listen to your heart,
it knows everything.

-Paulo Coelho

Keep SMILING.
It makes people wonder what you are up to.

-Becky Fowler Blackmon

Do not let your negative seeds grow
in your mental garden.

-Author unknown

All that YOU are LOOKING for you *ALREADY* are.

-Deepak Chopra

People always think that the most painful thing is losing the one you love in your life. The truth is, the most painful thing is losing yourself in the process of loving someone too much, forgetting that you are special too.

-Author unknown

YOU NEVER FIND YOURSELF
till you face the truth.

-Pearl Bailey

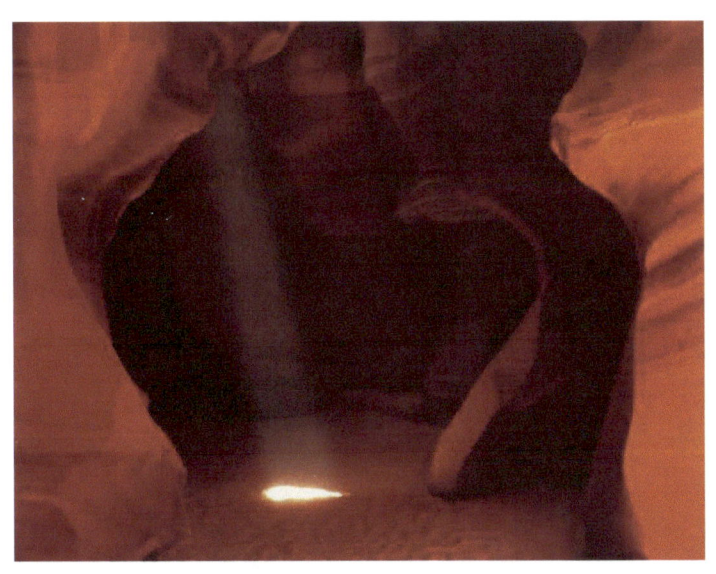

Failure is only the opportunity to begin again, only this time more wisely.

-Henry Ford

Nothing in life is impossible, the word itself says "I'M POSSIBLE".

-Audrey Hepburn

The first step towards change is
ACCEPTANCE.

-Author unknown

Drink your tea SLOWLY and reverently, as if it is the axis on which the world earth revolves - slowly, evenly, without rushing toward the future.

-Thich Nhat Hahn

A FRIEND IS LIKE A GOOD BRA,
DIFFICULT TO FIND, SUPPORTIVE,
LIFTS YOU
UP,
MAKES YOU FEEL GOOD, AND IS
ALWAYS CLOSE
TO
YOUR HEART.

-AUTHOR UNKNOWN

Even if I knew the world would go to pieces I would still plant my apple tree.

-Martin Luther

QUIET THE MIND,
and the soul will speak.

-Ma Jaya Sati Bhagavati

Don't matter how hard the past,
you can always begin anew.

-Buddha

Everything has a beauty,
but not everyone sees it.

-Confuscious

An interesting journey never follows a straight path.

-Marjan van den Belt

Look on every exit as being an entrance to somewhere else.

-Tom Stoppard

I have become my own version of an optimist.
If I can't make it through one door,
I'll go through another door,
or I'll make a door.

-Rabindranath Tagore

Let us not pray to be sheltered from dangers but to be fearless when facing them.

-Rabindranath Tagore

DON'T waste a minute not being happy. If one window closes, run to the next window- or break down a door.

-Brook Shields

A vision is not a static picture but a process that gets refined over time.

-Marjan van den Belt

Life is a song SING IT. Life is a game – PLAY IT. Life is a challenge – MEET IT. Life is a dream – REALIZE IT. Life is a sacrifice - offer it. Life is love – ENJOY IT.

-Sai Baba

Nobody can hurt me without my permission.

-Gandhi

Be still like a mountain.
Flow like a great *RIVER*.

-*Lao Tzu*

When the world wearies and society
fails to satisfy,
there is always the garden.

-Minnie Aumonier

Forgiveness is the greatest gift
you can give yourself.

-Maya Angelou

Every day IS a *second chance.*

-Author unknown

I have failed over and over again in my life, and that is why I succeed.

-Michael Jordon

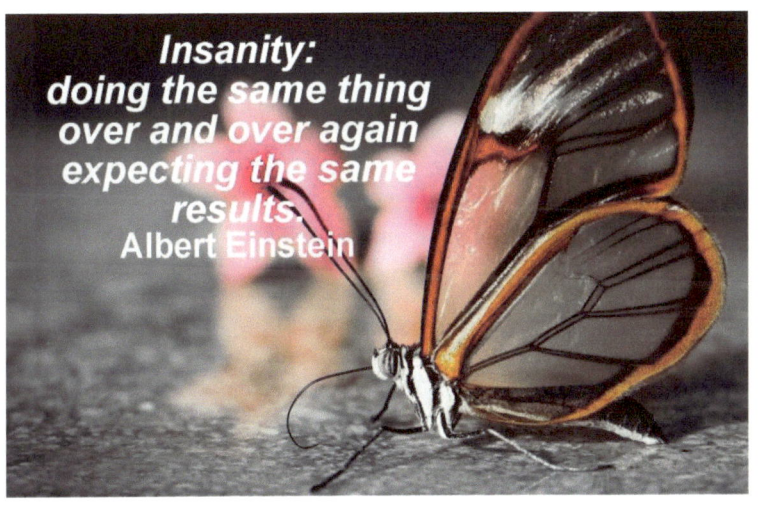

Courage does not always roar.
Sometimes courage is the quiet voice
at the end of the day saying, "I will
try again tomorrow."

-Mary Ann Radmacher

HAPPINESS IS FOUND WHEN YOU
stop comparing yourself to other PEOPLE.

-Author unknown

Enjoy
the little things of life
for one day you will realize
they were the BIG things.

-Robert Brault

Doing nothing is better than being busy doing nothing.

-Lao Tzu

Take a CHANCE.

-Author unknown

Knowing others is wisdom.
Knowing yourself is
ENLIGHTMENT.

-Lao Tzu

I hate to tell you, but NOW is all there ever is.

-Confucius

You cannot
CHANGE your journey,
If you are unwilling
to move at all.

-Allie Condie

Life is really *simple,* but we make it really complicated.

-Confucius

A crust eaten in peace is better than a banquet partaken in anxiety.

-Aesop

A person who never made a mistake never tried anything new.

-Albert Einstein

Change your thoughts and you change your world.

-Norman Vincent Peale

You can't do it all today,
but you CAN DO IT.

-Author Unknown

In the moment of crisis, the wise build bridges and the foolish build dams.

-Nigerian Proverb

Mindfulness is paying attention to the present moment with intention, While letting go of judgment, as if your life depends on it.

-Jon Kabat-Zinn

Each place is the right place--the place where I now am can be a sacred space.

-Ravi Ravindra

A SMOOTH SEA NEVER MADE A SKILLFUL *sailor*.

-English Proverb

Knowing how to YIELD is *strength*.

-*Lao Tzu*

People spend lots of time on doing things that make them unhappy. To cultivate joy spend time on what you like.

-Annie Kagan

Welcoming my loneliness, facing my shadows and falling in love with them and me was such a wonderful Heroes Journey, a path towards opening of my heart. *What a gift*!

-Fernando Pessoa

Lord grant me the serenity to accept the things I cannot change, the courage to change the things I can, and the wisdom to know the difference.

-Serenity Prayer, Karl Paul Reinhold Niebuhr

WE MUST NOT ALLOW THE CLOCK AND THE CALENDAR TO BLIND US TO THE FACT THAT EACH MOMENT OF LIFE IS A MIRACLE AND MYSTERY.

-H.G Wells

It isn't true that everyone should
follow one path.
Listen to your own truth.

-Ram Dass

In the end only three things matter: how much you loved, how gently you lived, and how gracefully you let go of things not meant for you.

-Buddha

Quotes Reference Table

Focus	See Pages
Mindfulness	p. 12, 13, 19, 23, 27, 30, 31, 34, 35, 39, 41, 51, 53, 54, 61, 71, 80, 89, 98
Fresh perspective	p. 14, 15, 68, 69, 70, 86, 95, 97
Comfort zone	p. 16, 42, 100, 106
Purpose	17, 52, 56, 60
Silence/Peace	p. 18, 19, 27, 44, 46, 54, 89, 99, 102, 105, 110
Be Positive/ Positive change	p. 19, 21, 26, 31, 76, 83, 95, 106, 107
Miracles	p. 78, 82
Planting new seeds/creating new possibilities	p. 20, 48, 50, 67, 72, 81, 85, 93
Joy	p. 22, 62, 64, 66, 87, 97, 98, 114
Friendship	p. 23, 75,
Transformation/Change	p. 28, 36, 56, 90

Focus	See Pages
Love	p. 29
Forgiveness	p. 92
Perfection	p. 31
Magnificence	p. 37, 38
Self-power	p. 43, 88 97, 101, 111
Surrender	p. 45, 109
Limitations	p. 47
Choice	p. 57
Rest	p. 58, 91
Courage	p. 59, 96, 100, 108, 83
Circumstances	p. 63
Intuition	p. 66
Negative thoughts	p. 67
Failure	P 71, 94, 112, 40
Acceptance	p. 73, 92, 113
Fearlessness	p. 83
The Journey	p. 80
The little things of life	p. 98
Simplicity	p. 104

My Mindful Quotes

My Mindful Quotes

My Mindful Quotes

My Mindful Quotes

My Mindful Quotes

My Mindful Quotes

My Mindful Quotes

My Mindful Quotes

My Mindful Quotes

My Mindful Quotes

My Mindful Quotes

My Mindful Quotes

My Mindful Quotes

My Mindful Quotes

My Mindful Quotes

My Mindful Quotes

My Mindful Quotes

My Mindful Quotes

My Mindful Quotes

My Mindful Quotes

Reference

Kabat-Zinn, J. (2006). Mindfulness for beginners. Louisville, Co: Sounds True

Picture Credits

Image 1. *Woman Meditating.* Photograph. May 15, 2014. http://www.inspiringnet.com
Image 2. *Water Drop.* Photograph. May 15, 2014. http.//www.wallpapertube.com
Image 3. Butterfly on Water drop. Photograph. May 15, 2014. http.//www.linewalls.com
Image 4. Affirmation. Omileye Achikeobi-Lewis. May 15, 2014
Image 5.*Man on Mountain.* Photograph. May 15, 2014. http.//www.wallpaper.com
Image 6. *Water.* Photograph. May 15, 2014. http.//www.ytz.com
Image 7. *Buddha.* Photograph. May 15, 2014. http.//www.wallpapergang.com
Image 8. *Moon. Photograph.* May 15, 2014. http.//www.wallpaperhq.com
Image 9. *Dandelion.* Photograph. May 15, 2014. http.//www.wallpaper.com
Image 10. *Sunset.* Photograph. May 15, 2014. http.//www.wallpaper.com
Image 11. *Dandelion Seed.* Photograph. May 15, 2014. http.//www.wallpaperz.com

Image 12. *Polar Bear.* Photograph. May 15, 2014. http.//www.wallpapertoon.com
Image 13. *Trees.* Photograph. May 15, 2014. http.//www.wallpapertoon.com
Image 14. *Buddha.* Photograph. May 15, 2014. http.//www.wallpaper.com
Image 15. *Woman by Water.* Photograph. May 15, 2014. http.//www.Inspiringwallpapers.com
Image 16. *Water.* Photograph. May 15, 2014. http.//www.Sciencelakes.com
Image 17. *Drops of Water.* Photograph. May 15, 2014. http.//www.widewallpapers.com
Image 18. *Drops of Water.* Photograph. May 15, 2014. http.//www.beautifulwallpaper.com
Image 19. *Hand Shape of Love Heart.* Photograph. May 15, 2014. http.//www.wallpaperswa.com
Image 20. *Blue Christmas Tree.* Photograph. May 15, 2014. http.//www.wallpaperswa.com
Image 21. *Puppy Dreaming Animal.* Photograph. May 15, 2014. http.//www.sw.com

Image 22. *Zen Stones*. Photograph. May 15, 2014. http.//www. wallgave.com
Image 23. Rays of Light Through Cloud. Photograph. May 15, 2014. http.//www. image.net
Image 24. *Hand Holding Love Heart*. Photograph. May 15, 2014. http.//www. widewallpaper.com
Image 25. *Butterfly Wings*. Photograph. May 15, 2014. http.//www. wallpapercraft.com
Image 26. *Lamp*. Photograph. May 15, 2014. http.//www. Gde.fon.com
Image 27. *Sunset Water*. Photograph. May 15, 2014. http.//www.wallpaper_ewebbb4.com
Image 28. *Surfing*. Photograph. May 15, 2014. http.//www.wallpapers.com
Image 29. *Hands of Light*. Photograph. May 15, 2014. http.//www.Desktopnexus.com
Image 30. Sleepy Bear. Photograph. May 15, 2014. http.//www.Desktopnexus.com
Image 31. *Blue Rocks Butterfly*. Photograph. May 15, 2014. http.//www.wallpapers.com
Image 32. *Woman in Field*. Photograph. May 15, 2014. http.//www.wallpapers.com

Image 33. Flower. Photograph. May 15, 2014. http.//www.wallpapers.com
Image 34. *Ship Sailing*. Photograph. May 15, 2014. http.//www.desk7.net
Image 35. *Water Butterfly*. Photograph. May 15, 2014. http.//www.wapaperedit.com
Image 36. Water Drop. Photograph. May 15, 2014. http.//www.wallsave.net
Image 37. Omi. *Affirmation*.
Image 38. *Dandelion in Sunset*. Photograph. May 15, 2014. http.//www.wallpapers_freereview.com
Image 39. *Doorway*. Photograph. May 15, 2014. http.//www.wallpaper4me.com
Image 40. *Blowing Dust*. Photograph. May 15, 2014. http.//www.scfoodfun.com
Image 41. *Setting Sun*. Photograph. May 15, 2014. http.//www.wallpaperapeggs.com
Image 42. Dandelion and *Water Drop*. Photograph. May 15, 2014. http.//www.wallpaperapeggs.com
Image 43. *Butterfly*. Photograph. May 15, 2014. http.//www.goodfon.com
Image 44. Miscellaneous *Notes*. Photograph. May 15, 2014. http.//www.inspiringwallpaper.com

Image 45. *Water Clouds*. Photograph. May 15, 2014. http.//www.wallvan.com
Image 46. *Heart*. Photograph. May 15, 2014. http.//www. wallpaper.net
Image 47. *Sleepy*. Photograph. May 15, 2014. http.//www.wallpaperhere.com
Image 48. *Love Heart*. Photograph. May 15, 2014. http.//www.inspiringwallpaper.net
Image 49. *Cute Kitty Kissing*. Photograph. May 15, 2014. http.//www.inspiringwallpaper.net
Image 50. *Cute Dog*. Photograph. May 15, 2014. http.//www.inspiringwallpaper.net
Image 51. Girl Valentine. Photograph. May 15, 2014. http.//www.inspiringwallpaper.net
Image 52. Sky. Photograph. May 15, 2014. http.//www.inspiringwallpaper.net
Image 53. Horse Running. Photograph. May 15, 2014. http.//www.inspiringwallpaper.net
Image 54. Love Heart Balloon. Photograph. May 15, 2014. http.//www.inspiringwallpaper.net

Image 55. Happy T.Shirt. Photograph. May 15, 2014.
http.//www.inspiringwallpaper.net
Image 56. Stones Colorful. Photograph. May 15, 2014.
http.//www.inspiringwallpaper.net
Image 57. Ocean Life. Photograph. May 15, 2014. http.//www.inspiringwallpaper.net
Image 58. Butterfly. Photograph. May 15, 2014. http.//www.inspiringwallpaper.net
Image 59. Flower Colorful Leaves. Photograph. May 15, 2014.
http.//www.inspiringwallpaper.net
Image 60. Light. Photograph. May 15, 2014.
http.//www.inspiringwallpaper.net
Image 61. Boat. Photograph. May 15, 2014.
http.//www.inspiringwallpaper.net
Image 62. Girl at Beach. Photograph. May 15, 2014.
http.//www.inspiringwallpaper.net
Image 63. Girl. Photograph. May 15, 2014.
http.//www.inspiringwallpaper.net
Image 64. Affirmation. Omileye Achikeobi-Lewis. May 15, 2014
Image 65. Tree. Photograph. May 15, 2014.
http.//www.inspiringwallpaper.net

Image 66. :Leaf Water. Photograph. May 15, 2014. http.//www.wallgang.com
Image 67. Flower and Water. Photograph. May 15, 2014. http.//www.inspiringwallpaper.net
Image 68. Castle. Photograph. May 15, 2014. http.//www.hdwallpaper.com
Image 69. Footsteps. Photograph. May 15, 2014. http.//www.desktopnexus.net
Image 70. Key Photograph. May 15, 2014. http.//www.desktopnexus.net
Image 71. Door. Photograph. May 15, 2014. http.//www.hdphoto.com
Image 72. Surf. Photograph. May 15, 2014. http.//www.hdphoto.com
Image 73. Dolphins. Photograph. May 15, 2014. http.//www.hdphoto.com
Image 74. Frosty Face. Photograph. May 15, 2014. http.//www.hdphoto.com
Image 75. Steps down to Place. Photograph. May 15, 2014. http.//www.datawallpaper.com
Image 76. Sunset Woman. Photograph. May 15, 2014. http.//www.hdwallpaper.com

Image 77. Silhouette Girl. Photograph. May 15, 2014. http.//www.listofimages.com
Image 78. Water Drop. Photograph. May 15, 2014. http.//www.wallpaper.com
Image 79. Butterfly. Photograph. May 15, 2014. http.//www.deviant.com
Image 80. Yellow Flower. Photograph. May 15, 2014. http.//www.wallpaperstock.net
Image 81. Book Page Love Heart. Photograph. May 15, 2014. http.//www.inspiringwallpaper.net
Image 82. Woman Meditating. Photograph. May 15, 2014. http.//www.desktopnexus.com
Image 83. Tigers. Photograph. May 15, 2014. http.//www.bestwallpaper.com
Image 84. Butterfly. Photograph. May 15, 2014. http.//www.2bp_blogspot.com
Image 85. Lion in Sunset. Photograph. May 15, 2014.
http.//www.crazyfrankenstein.com
http.//www.crazyfrankenstein.com
Image 86. Ramadan Moon. Photograph. May 15, 2014.
http.//www.7culloso.com.com

Image 87. Miscellaneous Letter. Photograph. May 15, 2014. http.//www.vastavki.com

Image 88. Lantern. Photograph. May 15, 2014. http.//www.goodfon_su.com

Image 89. Cat Height. Photograph. May 15, 2014. http.//www.hdwallpaper.com

Image 90. Leaf Water. Photograph. May 15, 2014. http.//www.hdwallpaper.com

Image 91. Flower. Photograph. May 15, 2014. http.//www.hdwallpaper.com

Image 92. Polar Bear. Photograph. May 15, 2014. http.//www.hdwallpaper.com

Image 93. Peacock Feather. Photograph. May 15, 2014. http.//www.wallpapercraft.com

Image 94. Shell. Photograph. May 15, 2014. http.//www.wallpapers.com

Image 95. Flower. Photograph. May 15, 2014. http.//www.hdwallpapers.com

Image 96. Eagle. Photograph. May 15, 2014. http.//www.wallpapers.com

Image 97. Flower. Photograph. May 15, 2014. http.//www.alpacoders.com

Image 98. Yellow Flower. Photograph. May 15, 2014. http.//www.customity.com

Image 99. Yellow Flower. Photograph. May 15, 2014. http.//www.hdwallpapers.com
Image 100. Budding Flower. Photograph. May 15, 2014. http.//www.walkco.com
Image 101. Colorful Water Drops. Photograph. May 15, 2014. http.//www.walkco.com
Image 102. Beach. Photograph. May 15, 2014. http.//www.walkco.com
Image 103. Chicks. Photograph. May 15, 2014. http.//www.walkco.com
Image 104. Boat. Photograph. May 15, 2014. http.//www.wallvan.com
Image 105. Field of Grass. Photograph. May 15, 2014. http.//www.wallvan.com
Image 106. Magic Horse. Photograph. May 15, 2014. http.//www.wallvan.com
Image 107. Cuddly Bear. Photograph. May 15, 2014. http.//www.wallvan.com
Image 108. Gebera Flowers. Photograph. May 15, 2014. http.//www.wallvan.com

www.ingramcontent.com/pod-product-compliance
Lightning Source LLC
Chambersburg PA
CBHW041625220426
43663CB00001B/13